AN ARTIST'S JOURNEY

From The City to The Peak

PAULINE SHEARSTONE AYA FRSA

Pauline, sketching outdoors.
(Photograph N. Bird)

Sheffield born artist and writer, Pauline Shearstone, has enjoyed a varied painting and writing career. Her previous five books covering local history have been very successful.

Pauline's painting commissions have been no less impressive with a series of eighteen watercolours for *HMS Sheffield*, paintings for the Yorkshire Regiments, and a Nobel Prize Winner.

For many years Pauline has been a watercolour tutor, running both private courses and painting holidays as well as teaching for the University of Sheffield.

More recently her work can be seen in *Leisure Painter* magazine for which she has regularly contributed.

She is a Fellow of the prestigious RSA and is an Associate of the Yorkshire Artists.

Cover Illustration: *Chatsworth* watercolour

An Artist's Journey
From The City to The Peak

This book is an invitation to pack up your paints and join me on, *An Artist's Journey*

written and illustrated by
PAULINE SHEARSTONE AYA FRSA

© 1998 Pauline Shearstone

Published by The Hallamshire Press

The Hallamshire Press is an imprint of
Interleaf Productions Limited
Broom Hall
Sheffield S10 2DR
England

Typeset by Interleaf Productions Limited
Printed in Singapore

Every care has been taken to reproduce colour accurately but, due to the limitations of the processes involved, the colours reproduced may not match exactly those of the original works.

All rights reserved. No part of this publication may be reproduced, stored in a retrieval system, or transmitted, in any form or by any means, electronic, mechanical, photocopying, recording or otherwise, without the prior permission in writing of the publishers.

British Library Cataloguing in Publication Data:
A catalogue record for this book is available from the British Library

ISBN 1 874718 33 4

Dedicated to my husband Walter and son Timothy for their constant help and encouragement and whose sense of humour I would not be without!

Other books by the author:
 Sheffield Sketches including Norton and the Chantrey Story. (1980)
 Portraits of the Cutlers' Hall (An illustrated guide book). (1983)
 Gleadless from Village to Suburb. (1985)
 Old Gleadless: Just a little country village. (1989)
 J.W. Mottershaw's Sheffield: His life and work. (1994)

I should like to thank Pauline Climpson at The Hallamshire Press for giving me such freedom in the design of this book and for all her advice and enthusiasm. I am grateful too to Keith Farnsworth, an accomplished author, and his wife, Linda, for their encouragement. I appreciate the help of Janet Barnes, who kindly wrote the foreword, and my son Timothy who designed the maps and gave advice. A special thank you to all my students, past and present, for their support and friendship. May they read the book from cover to cover and find that it is just what they wanted!

FOREWORD

There is a long British tradition of painting in watercolour that has deepened the national appreciation of both landscape and art. The practice is widespread and many people find enjoyment and increased visual awareness through it. Indeed, John Ruskin, the great Victorian writer and artist, was a great advocate of the benefits to be gained from watercolour painting.

This publication, in line with this tradition, offers a guide to scenes of visual interest whether they be of the industrial heritage of the City of Sheffield or of The Peak District. Pauline Shearstone, who has made studies of these areas over the years, has brought her talents, as an artist and Art Tutor, together in this book.

Pauline takes us on a journey from the centre of a large industrial city on through the suburbs and out into The Peak District. Various painting techniques are introduced and explained and there are also notes of interest on the chosen subjects. Whether making your own attempts at watercolour painting or simply enjoying the collection of illustrations, *An Artist's Journey* will increase the pleasure to be gained through looking. There is always more to a watercolour or drawing than the wealth of detail in a photograph—there is, in the human mark, a record of enjoyment.

Janet Barnes

Janet Barnes
Exhibitions and Collections Manager

THE RUSKIN GALLERY

Norfolk Street. Map reference 1

This award winning gallery on Norfolk Street was opened in 1985 in a former wine merchant's premises. The Victorian social and art theorist, John Ruskin, set up the Guild of St George in 1871 to house his collection of drawings, prints, watercolours and architectural plaster casts which he hoped would inspire the working class to understand and appreciate what is lovely in nature.

The collection, once contained in a house in Walkley, belongs to the Guild but is on long term loan to Sheffield. The exhibitions are either selected from the collection or are based on topics which relate to the understanding of Ruskin's ideas.

The Ruskin, as it is known locally, has some interesting features, including the staircase and balustrade, by Guisseppe Lund, leading to the upstairs gallery, the watercolour inscriptions of Ruskin quotes, and David Kindersley's (once apprenticed to Eric Gill) fine lettering on slate slabs.

The small adjoining *Ruskin Craft Gallery* which opened in 1988, holds exhibitions and displays of contemporary craft work and complements the art gallery's fine reputation.

Telephone: 0114 273 5299 for opening details.

The Ruskin Gallery (10 × 8) line and wash
on a smooth 140lb watercolour paper.

ILLUSTRATIONS

CONTENTS

INTRODUCTION

The idea for this book came from my students who requested me to publish a book that they could take home with them after my painting courses finished and refer to later, not only for advice but, hopefully, to gain inspiration!

Selecting just a few of the many places that I have visited and painted over the years has proved to be very difficult. There are so many good painting locations in The City, if you look for them, and in the countryside of The Peak. Anyone who has visited the Peak District does not need me to tell them how beautiful the landscape is.

For the purposes of the book the locations had to be limited. In order to offer a varied selection of places for the artist to paint and the tourist to visit, some old favourites have been left out and others have been included. I am sorry if I have left out your favourite place.

An Artist's Journey relates to a journey in the physical sense of the word, by actually travelling to, and painting at, various locations. It is also a journey of discovery for the artist, whether as a beginner or an improver, starting with 'Beginners' Basics' and progressing onto 'Watercolour Landscape Techniques'.

Project Pages are included along the way to help you master certain simple (did I say simple?) techniques before journeying on to more difficult ones. These are meant to be tried and tested before attempting something new. Towards the end of the book, near the 'Journey's End', the projects are more complicated.

To complement the book, I have included historical notes together with my personal impressions of the times I have spent painting outdoors in enjoyable company.

This book is an invitation to pack up your paints and join me on *An Artist's Journey*.

Pauline Shearstone

September 1998

MATERIALS

Choosing the art materials you need in order to start painting can be a little daunting. To help with this problem I am listing the art materials that I use, you may wish to try these for yourself to get you started.

SELECTING YOUR COLOURS

I use Artists' quality paints in tubes, preferring to squeeze out generous helpings of paint into my watercolour palette. For the beginner, if cost is important, the Student quality range of paints may be advisable as they are less expensive.

Artists vary in the colours they use and the 'palette' you adopt becomes a matter of personal taste—like choosing the colour of the clothes you wear. I tend not to use black or Chinese white and prefer to mix my own greens.

The colours I use are shown overleaf, you may like to add to these or change them as you progress.

WATERCOLOUR PALETTES

For indoor use I have a large, white palette which has good mixing areas and empty colour wells which I fill with paint and keep topping-up.

If the paint dries out, moisten it with a wet bristle brush to soften it before you start to paint.

When painting outdoors I have a palette with a lid which closes over the box and prevents wet paint from running into your bag. The Winsor & Newton Field Box is another outdoor palette which I find ideal as it is small enough to fit into your pocket.

MY WATERCOLOUR PALETTE

1. Cobalt Blue
2. French Ultramarine
3. Winsor Blue (red shade)
4. Payne's Gray (Winsor & Newton Artists' Quality)
5. Cerulean Blue
6. Cadmium Red
7. Rose Madder
8. Lemon Yellow
9. Raw Sienna
10. Cadmium Yellow
11. Burnt Sienna
12. Burnt Umber
13. Light Red
14. Indian Red

BRUSHES

Sable brushes are the best but they are expensive. Synthetic brushes which are on the market are good and inexpensive. To protect your paintbrushes when travelling, pop them into a brush case. When not in use, store them upright in a jar to allow them to dry out.

My basic brush selection:

I tend to use Pro Arte brushes which I find are excellent and very durable.

When giving so many painting demonstrations throughout the year, I have to have brushes that last!

Prolene Pro Arte flat one stroke brushes, 1/2-inch to a 3/4-inch (Series 106) for painting large areas and washes.

Two or three rounded brushes a No. 8 and a No. 10 or No. 12 (Series 101).

A rigger brush No. 2 which is excellent for adding final details.

These are the least number of brushes that I use, and that you will need to start.

PAPER

I always use a good quality watercolour paper preferring not to struggle with poor paper as it makes painting even more difficult. I use various paper weights ranging from a 260lb to 140lb, and from a rough textured surface to a smooth.

Bockingford watercolour paper is an excellent, economical paper which can withstand many different watercolour techniques. It is a paper I use time and again and one I can certainly recommend for both beginner and the more advanced painter.

Bockingford also make five tinted papers; grey, cream, eggshell, oatmeal and blue. You can use these coloured papers in the normal traditional watercolour manner or try experimenting on them with pen & ink, gouache or watercolour pencils.

Watercolour paper can be bought in three surfaces:
Rough paper has a rough surface
Hot Pressed (HP) is smooth
NOT paper has a medium texture

Paper weights range from:
Very thick, for example 300lb, to thinner lighter paper such as 90lb. The lighter the paper, the more tendency it has to buckle when wet, so it is advisable to stretch the paper onto a board first before using. I buy full sheets of paper and cut them into whatever size I require, rather than using a standard size sheet in a watercolour pad.

SKETCHBOOKS

Sketchbooks contain cartridge paper which is meant primarily for drawing, although a light colour wash can be added. For outdoor sketching I use sketchbooks from pocket-size A6 up to the larger A4 size. Indoors, I use single sheets of cartridge paper for larger sketches.

MATERIALS CHECKLIST

DRAWING BOARD

Include a 16 inch × 12 inch board, or thick card, on which to attach your paper. Use double-sided masking tape on the reverse side of the paper.

WATER POTS

For outdoor work I use a plastic collapsible water pot, one which folds flat after use, and a screw-top water container which I fill before starting the journey! Use one or two large water jars indoors.

TISSUES & RAGS

Paper tissues are very useful, not only for cleaning brushes and palettes, but also for lifting out colour in a painting. Cloth rags are required for cleaning up bigger messes!

PENCILS

Have a selection of pencils graded from F, HB, B, 2B to 4B.

Include a pencil eraser and a sharpener. Graphite Aquarelle pencils, available in grades, very soft, soft and medium are invaluable for tonal sketching (see 'Sketching Techniques').

MASKING FLUID

Required for blocking out white areas and adding textural effects to a painting. For scratching out white areas, try a pen knife, or your finger nail which you grow long for that purpose!

EASELS

A table easel is useful for indoor work. For outdoor painting I have two easels. A metal one which I stand up to and a seat easel which, as its name implies, is one I use sitting down. However, a small stool to sit on and a board resting on your knee is adequate for most people.

A WATERPROOF CARRYING BAG

Choose a waterproof bag that stands flat so that your palette lays flat in the bottom of the bag without disturbing all the wet paint. Have one with pockets, for your water container and other bits and pieces, and ensure there is sufficient space for all your art materials and camera.

OUTDOOR CLOTHING

Include a hat, waterproof clothing, umbrella and strong shoes, on your list.

When all your painting preparations are complete, you are ready to start your painting journey!

Learning to mix your paints is so important and is one of the joys of watercolour painting as so many lovely effects can be made by experimenting with colour but, to begin with, you must understand simple colour theory. Try out the following colour mixing exercises.

PRIMARIES AND SECONDARIES

Red, yellow and blue are the **three primary colours** and when two of these are mixed you will have a second colour. The yellow with blue makes a green; the yellow and red produce orange; and blue and red together create a purple. So the **secondaries** are green, orange and purple.

MAKING A COLOUR WHEEL

Make your own colour wheel by painting the three primary colours, in segments of a circle, using watercolour paper. Add water and mix the colours together to produce the secondaries. With more water, blend the colours out so they become paler on the circle's outer edges. To make a colour paler in watercolour painting add more water to your mix. To produce a stronger colour use more pigment and less water.

Colour Wheel
Colours used: *Cadmium Yellow*, *French Ultramarine* and *Rose Madder*.

A. COMPLEMENTARY MIXING

 Rose Madder (red)   green

 Cadmium Yellow   violet

French Ultramarine   orange

COMPLEMENTARIES
The three primaries have a **complementary colour**, or an opposite, created by mixing the two remaining primaries.

The complementary colour of red is green which is derived from the two primaries of blue and yellow. Yellow and violet, and blue and orange lie opposite each other on the colour wheel and are complementaries.

B. TERTIARIES (FROM LEFT TO RIGHT)

red orange   yellow orange   yellow green   blue green   blue violet   red violet

TERTIARIES
By mixing a primary and a secondary colour together a **tertiary colour** is produced. A red mixed with an orange becomes red-orange; yellow + orange = yellow/orange; yellow + green = yellow/green; blue + green = blue/green; blue + violet = blue/violet; and red + violet produces red/violet.

C. WARM AND COOL COLOURS

red, orange, yellow = warm   blue, green, violet = cold

WARM & COOL COLOURS
Reds, oranges and yellows are found to be **warm colours** while the **cool** ones are usually blue, green and violet. Some colours however, e.g. lemon yellow, are classed as cold, and Burnt Sienna added to a green makes it a warm green.

The basic skill of watercolour painting is applying washes.
To apply colour evenly over an area of paper a **Flat Wash** is used.

THE FLAT WASH

To begin with slope your board at an angle. This will keep the wash running downwards.

1. Mix one colour (Cobalt Blue) in your mixing well, sufficient to cover the area you wish to paint. It is better to mix too much than run the risk of running out of paint half way through a wash!

2. Using your ½-inch wash brush, dip into your mix and sweep the colour across the top of your **dry paper** from left to right.

3. Go back to the left and start again, picking up the little trickle of paint that has accumulated at the bottom of the first stroke. Your second brush stroke should overlap the first by just enough to gather the surplus wash.

4. Continue repeating this process until you have covered your paper with an area of even colour.

A SIMPLE SKY WASH

When you have mastered painting a flat wash, try painting a simple sky by following the method shown here.

In traditional watercolour, applying washes is required to obtain various colour effects. For example when a blue flat wash is applied over a yellow wash it produces a green.

1. Apply a flat wash of Cobalt Blue over your dry paper.

2. While the colour is still wet, use a tissue and dab out the colour to reveal white areas. These areas should suggest clouds in a blue sky and not flying saucers!

3. Suggest a foreground by sweeping your brush along the bottom of your picture.

A GRADED OR GRADUATED WASH

This wash starts with strong colour at the top and gradually pales out to the colour of the paper.

1. Again, tilt your board at an angle and mix a quantity of a single colour.

2. You can either dampen your paper first or leave it dry, depending on the effect that you require.

3. When you are happy with your mix, load your wash brush with paint and run a band of colour along the top of the paper.

4. Next, swiftly dip your brush into **clean** water and repeat the stroke, slightly overlapping the first stroke (as you did in the flat wash).

5. Repeat this process adding more water and gradually weakening the original colour until it merges with the colour of the paper.

This diluted wash is suitable for water and skies.

A graded wash

A landscape using a graded wash

THE VARIEGATED WASH

A variegated wash is when two or three colours are merged together and is great for adding atmosphere to a painting.

1. Mix three colours in three containers or wells. Use blue, yellow and red for the purpose of this exercise. The colours can be of varying strengths if you wish (by adding more or less water).

2. **Dampen** your paper with your wash brush. This will help the colours to blend.

3. Start at the top of your paper and lay a flat wash of blue.

4. While your paper is still wet, lay your second colour (yellow) and then your third (red).

5. The edges of the colours should merge into one another.

Experiment with this wash for, although it may not be the simplest one to do, it is always unpredictable and gives a very Turner-like effect to your painting!

A variegated wash using Cobalt Blue, Yellow Ochre & Cadmium Red

Some colours are transparent while others are opaque and conceal the colour underneath. Overlaying colour is very effective when making a wash darker, or when used with pen and wash when the transparent colours allow the ink to show through.

Winsor colours tend to be transparent e.g. *Winsor Red* and *Winsor Yellow*. *Alizarin Crimson* and *Raw Sienna* are too, while *Yellow Ochre* and *Cadmium Red* are opaque colours.

Discover which ones are transparent by overlaying colours over a black Indian ink line. Those that cover up the line are opaque those that do not are transparent.

Test strips

Test which colours are transparent by overlaying strips of colour, as shown in figures 1, 2 & 3:

1. My first wash was *Cadmium Yellow* (opaque) superimposed with *Rose Madder* (transparent) followed by a wash of *French Ultramarine* (transparent).

2. *Cobalt Blue* was painted first and was then overlapped with *Cadmium Yellow* and *Rose Madder*.

3. *Rose Madder*, the transparent colour, is completely covered by the opaque yellow.

OVERLAYING COLOURS

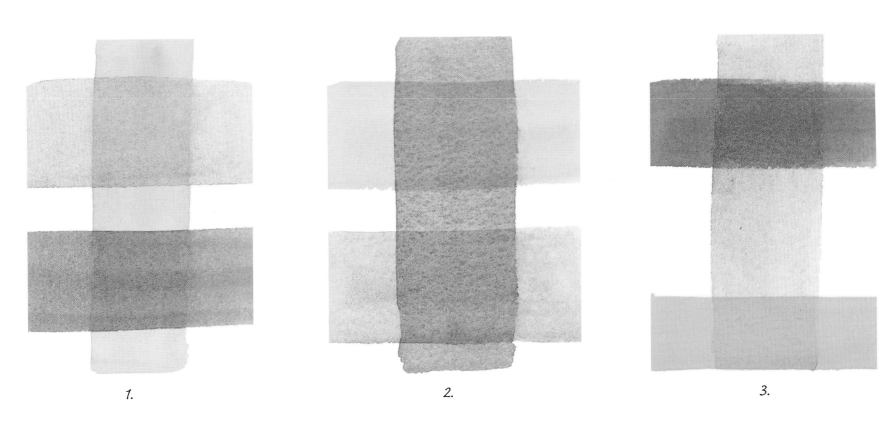

1.   2.   3.

A
CITY
JOURNEY

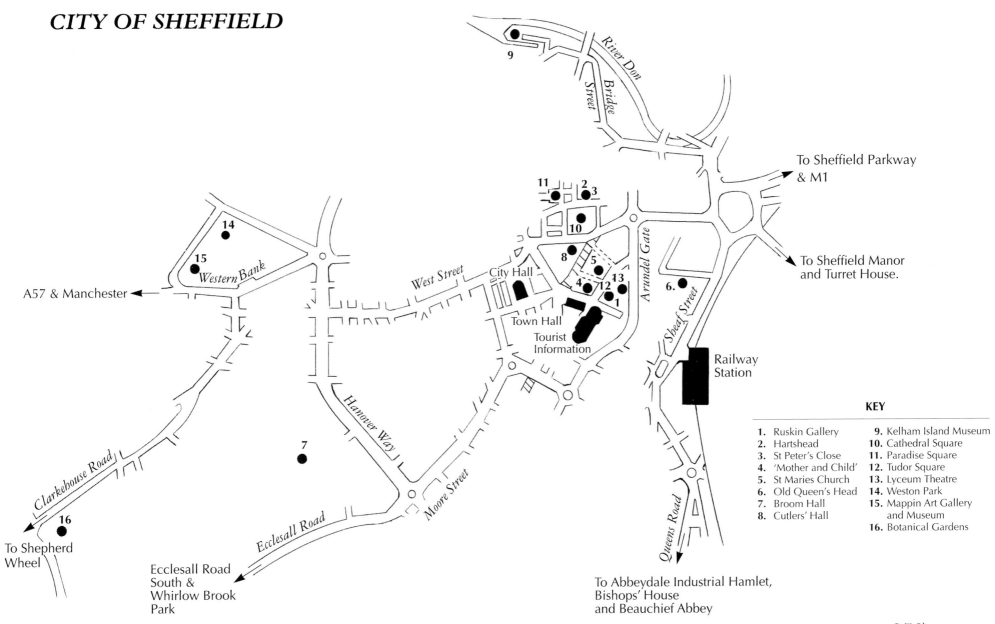

CITY OF SHEFFIELD

River Don

Bridge Street

To Sheffield Parkway & M1

To Sheffield Manor and Turret House.

Arundel Gate

West Street

City Hall

Town Hall

Tourist Information

Western Bank

A57 & Manchester

Sheaf Street

Railway Station

Hanover Way

Clarkehouse Road

Moore Street

Ecclesall Road

Queens Road

To Shepherd Wheel

Ecclesall Road South & Whirlow Brook Park

To Abbeydale Industrial Hamlet, Bishops' House and Beauchief Abbey

KEY

1. Ruskin Gallery
2. Hartshead
3. St Peter's Close
4. 'Mother and Child'
5. St Maries Church
6. Old Queen's Head
7. Broom Hall
8. Cutlers' Hall
9. Kelham Island Museum
10. Cathedral Square
11. Paradise Square
12. Tudor Square
13. Lyceum Theatre
14. Weston Park
15. Mappin Art Gallery and Museum
16. Botanical Gardens

© T. Shearstone

SKETCHING TECHNIQUES

City sketching is not for the faint-hearted—people love to watch someone sketching! So a small pocket sketchbook and a camera are always useful aids when working in the city.

Develop the habit of using a sketchbook. A rough sketch drawn 'on the spot' is worth many photographs. However small the sketch it can often be developed into a painting later.

Rough sketches and detailed drawings

My sketches usually suggest ideas for a future painting. Composition and tone are worked out in these 'roughs'.

Hartshead *and* St Peter's Close, Hartshead *sketches were drawn with a 2B pencil. The lean and line of the buildings were more interesting to me than drawing in every brick! What you leave out of a sketch is just as important as what you put in. Learn to simplify.*

My drawings tend to be more finished pieces and include more attention to detail.

Hartshead (8 × 5) pencil

26

Pauline Shearstone

MATERIALS

For sketching I use a range of pencils from HB to 4B, HB for fine detail, up to 4B which is a very soft pencil and produces a darker, thicker line. I use a 2B pencil when drawing for my paintings. A heavier pencil leaves too much graphite on the paper and can look muddy when a watercolour is painted over it.

Taped sketchbooks containing cartridge paper, ranging from A3 to A5 size fit nicely into my pocket.

For detailed drawings I use sheets of good quality drawing paper which can take a light watercolour wash if required.

WASH DRAWINGS

Aquarelle pencils and wash drawings

To produce a wash drawing I draw with a Berol Karismacolor graphite pencil. The *soft* and *medium* grades are excellent pencils and can be used dry as a normal pencil or you can wash over the pencil with water to produce a wash drawing. The heavier the pencil the darker the tones become.

My drawings *Mother and Child* and the *Sheffield Manor Ruins* are two examples where I have used this wash drawing technique. Practise drawing as it will give you confidence in your painting. Get into the sketchbook habit.

St Peter's Close, Hartshead ($8^{1}/_{2} \times 4$) pencil

GEORGE FULLARD'S *Mother and Child*

Just off Norfolk Street is Upper Chapel Yard which is a little haven where one can sit undisturbed.

Bronzes by the late George Fullard, the Sheffield sculptor born in the 1920s, are sited here. I enjoy Fullard's work and feel his Mother and Child captures the restrained effort of a mother wrestling to keep her child on her knee. In the 1950s his drawings and sculpture featured the human figure and, in particular, mothers, babies, and children. Fullard, 'never forgot his working class roots...which fuelled his fertile imagination...until his untimely death in 1973'.[1]

Another familiar Fullard bronze is his Walking Man (1957).

1. *George Fullard: A Fastidious Primitive.* Yorkshire Sculpture Park, 1997.

Mother and Child (12 × 5) Aquarelle pencil wash

This wash drawing was done on smooth 140lb Winsor & Newton watercolour paper, using a soft grade Aquarelle pencil which was later washed over with water. I concentrated on the seated figures and tapered the drawing leaving out surrounding buildings and the other bronzes. The Town Hall, towering above, signifies Fullard's connection with the city. This drawing was done later in the studio using several sketches drawn on the spot.

Aquarelle pencil can be also be used in combination with ink, as illustrated in St Marie's Church from Upper Chapel Yard. *St Marie's (Map reference 5) the elaborately decorated 19th-century Catholic Cathedral, is situated in Norfolk Row a little pedestrianised street just off Fargate.*

DRAWING IN PEN AND INK

TECHNIQUES

Pen and ink drawing complements watercolour very well. Used as a quick sketch or as a detailed drawing it can be very effective. Rembrandt produced sepia ink and wash sketches as studies for his paintings, but the economy of line and tone make them finished works of art.

LINE AND MASS

Line, or outline, drawing concentrates on line work alone, unlike mass drawing which is executed in a wash, with mass and tone being the major factors and line making no contribution. Drawings are usually produced with a combination of line and mass.

MATERIALS

A simple pen holder and a nib which you dip into a bottle of black Indian ink are all you need to get you started. Dip pens, as they are called, vary from fine mapping pens, which are ideal for linear sketches, to Gillott drawing pens which give thicker strokes. Inks vary too, and are available in different colours. To prevent smudging when water is added to your ink drawing, make sure your ink is waterproof first. Dip pens tend to be unpredictable when it comes to varying strokes and the ink flow can run out when drawing a line but I love their unpredictability. The dip pen, used with black or sepia ink, has become the traditional hallmark of pen drawings over the years.

St Marie's Church from Upper Chapel Yard (10 × 6¹/₂) Aquarelle pencil and ink

MODERN PENS

There are many types of modern pens on the market, including felt-tip pens, fountain pens and technical pens. One of my favourite pens is the Rotring Artpen EF (extra fine) the ink is water soluble and works with a replaceable ink cartridge. This is ideal for outdoor work and is so compact that it fits into your pocket along with a small sketchbook. Adding water to the finished sketch creates a good tonal effect. I make my own pens too, by sharpening sticks to a point and then using them in the same way as a dip pen.

PAPER

Drawing paper, and a smooth (HP) watercolour paper are the best to work on, as rough watercolour paper can cause a nib to dig in shooting ink everywhere! Tinted papers are worth trying too.

For a watercolour wash always paint on a 140lb watercolour paper otherwise when the wash is added the paper will buckle.

LINE & WASH DRAWING

When ink is used in combination with watercolour, the technique is called line and wash. If you wish to have more ink detail than colour, then draw with your ink first (make sure it is waterproof ink) then add colour. On the other hand should you only want a suggestion of line, then paint first then add ink later. Transparent watercolours (see Project Page 22) are the best to use as they allow the ink to show through, opaque colours do not.

I find pen and wash ideal for detailed illustrations and quick sketching—try it for yourself.

A Few Pointers
1. Apply ink over a 'lost' weak watercolour to strengthen it.
2. Draw with a pen directly onto your paper without any primary drawing. This will sharpen your observational powers and teach you to draw with the minimum of lines.
3. Work on a tinted paper and add white gouache for the highlights.
4. Try a combination of ink and watercolour for line and wash.
5. Experiment with various pens, coloured inks and papers. Discover what fascinating effects can be achieved.

HISTORICAL BUILDINGS

Sheffield Manor Ruins (4 × 11) wash drawing

The irregular shapes of the ruins, silhouetted against the skyline, are all that remain of this once splendid residence.

SHEFFIELD MANOR
Manor Lane

Every city has its buildings of historical interest and special merit and none more so than the ruins of Sheffield Manor, situated on the south east of the city on Manor Lane. This area was once a deer park and was where the hunting lodge belonging to the Earls of Shrewsbury was situated. Later, this mediaeval building was enlarged 'in the 16th century by stages to a more splendid mansion'.[1] the remains of which we see today. Famous visitors to the Manor include Cardinal Wolsey, in 1529, and Mary Queen of Scots who spent a lengthy time in Sheffield, some 14 years, as a prisoner both here and at Sheffield Castle.

1. *How it was then. Introducing Sheffield History.*

Suggestions are that the Turret House built in 1574 and the only roofed building now remaining, was constructed specially to house Mary. It is questionable, however, since the house was sited on the boundary wall and such an important prisoner would, 'more likely to have been kept in the main house now in ruins'.[1] The Manor, positioned high above the city, leads one to imagine Mary enjoying the view of Sheffield Park from the Turret House roof before retiring 'to the richly decorated upper rooms for refreshment and shelter'.[2]

1. *How it was then. Introducing Sheffield History.*
2. *Sheffield Manor.* Leaflet.

OLD QUEEN'S HEAD
Pond Hill. Map reference 6

From the Sheffield Manor we travel down into the city centre where we find Sheffield's oldest domestic building set in rather unusual surroundings. Here, alongside the Sheffield Interchange, or Pond Street Bus Station as it is known, is the *Old Queen's Head*.

There is a link between the Manor and this building which its modern environment belies. Once this 15th-century half-timbered building was referred to as 'The Hawle at the Poandes' and was the laundry to the Manor. It was surrounded by fields which housed the fishing ponds (hence the name Pond Street) which belonged to the Manor. The building has an intriguing past with its fair share of stories of ghosts and of secret tunnels which supposedly reach the Manor.

The Tudors loved building tunnels!

From its early idyllic setting, with chickens roaming past the door and children playing outside on a dusty road, as portrayed in old prints, this building has seen many changes.

In 1736 it was much larger, with projecting wings and a large garden, and was known as the *Queen's Head Hotel*.

By the mid-19th century the original gable end was demolished to make way for road widening in Pond Hill then, after many years of deterioration, it was restored and renovated in 1949.

This Grade II* listed building is now a modern public house and as such one can view the interior as well as the exterior of this attractive building.

Old Queen's Head
Pond Street (8 × 6) line and wash

Pond Street is a busy area where people rush about and board buses and coaches for various destinations so, as you can imagine, drawing here was not easy. I made several 'on the spot' sketches but backed them up by taking many photographs in case I needed to refer to them later for extra detail.

Back in the studio, I started my drawing with a 2B pencil on a smooth, 140lb, watercolour paper. I intended the illustration to be a line and wash drawing so I did not overdo the ink work. I introduced watercolour to the sky with Cobalt Blue. French Ultramarine was used for the roofs and windows, followed by a mix of Cobalt Blue and Light Red for the shadows.

The ink came last, the black timbers being drawn in with my Artpen. The rest of the sketch was left in pencil so that it would not detract from the main building. To add extra colour to certain areas, such as the shadows and windows, I added a few strokes with my watercolour pencils but kept them dry.

- Pauline Shearstone -

BISHOPS' HOUSE

Norton Lees Lane, Meersbrook Park

Leaving the Old Queen's Head behind us we journey on to Norton Lees Lane where, at the top of Meersbrook Park, overlooking a marvellous panoramic view of the city is Bishops' House, Sheffield's best surviving example of a timber-framed building.

Built around 1500, it was a typical home of a wealthy yeoman farmer. The Blythe family owned the house at one time and its name is derived from the fact that two of William Blythe's sons became Bishops, one of Salisbury, the other of Coventry and Lichfield.

The house has passed through many stages of building before arriving at what we see today. After the Civil War, with timber being scarce, a two-storey stone extension was built. By 1753 the property was sold and the house was then divided into two dwellings with each wing being a self-contained unit. The barns and outbuildings were demolished in 1886 and, when Meersbrook Park was formed in the same year, the house came to be occupied by council employees until 1974.

After a complete restoration Bishops' House opened as a City Museum in 1976. It is a very attractive, 'living' Museum with interesting displays and authentic furniture befitting a prosperous yeoman's home.

Open: Wednesday–Saturday 10am–4.30pm, Sunday 11am–4.30pm. Telephone: 0114 255 7701

Bishops' House, Meersbrook Park (6 × 10) pen and ink

One of the elements of a successful pen drawing is contrast. This building with its black and white timbers makes it an ideal subject for pen and ink work. Whereas in watercolour contrast is achieved with colour, in pen work tone is the key factor. I have not included cross-hatching here but have drawn in heavy lines with a broad Gillott's nib to suggest varying textures. I used a stippling effect for the foreground grass, while the stark background trees were drawn in with a fine nib which contrasted against the strong lines of the building. Indian ink does take some time to dry but a good solid black is achieved.

Pauline Shearstone

BROOM HALL
Broomhall Road. Map reference 7

Broom Hall, part of the Broomhall Conservation Area, is one of Sheffield's most important ancient buildings, with the earliest part being built in the 1500s. Once a large estate, many notable people have lived here including the Reverend James Wilkinson, Vicar of Sheffield from 1754–1805, who, while serving as a JP, saw the building of the East wing, and witnessed the scene, in 1791, of a riotous mob who tried unsuccessfully to burn down the Hall in protest at his harsh sentences. Over the years the Hall has undergone various changes of ownership but its elegant facade still remains. The front and the east wing can be seen from the road but the original 16th-century west wing, complete with its gable end and square oriel window, overlooks the rear garden. The Hall and grounds are now private property.

Broom Hall is a Grade II* listed building standing in spacious grounds with a long driveway leading up to it. After the threat of demolition, it was completely restored by the designer David Mellor who lived there and made it the base for his cutlery company before moving to Hathersage. Today, it houses several offices and is the headquarters of The Hallamshire Press

Broom Hall West Wing (12½ × 8) line and watercolour

My very loose watercolour worked well on this smooth 140lb watercolour paper. Perhaps this painting should have been executed in pen and ink but I found broad washes of light greens and browns (i.e. siennas and umbers) followed by warm shadow colours of Light Red and Cobalt Blue more suitable. A light touch with an Artpen completed the painting.

Broom Hall (9 × 14) pen and ink

I chose a 140lb Bockingford (NOT) watercolour
paper for this drawing as I had intended to
introduce some watercolour later. However, the
intricate detail would have been lost if watercolour
had been added, so it was left as a pen and ink
illustration. The large tree on the right gives scale to
the picture, while the dark background trees contrast
against the light tones of the building. To achieve
fine lines and a really dense black, I used a medium
sized nib, with black ink.

- Broom Hall -

Doorway at Broom Hall

(8¼ × 3) pencil and coloured pencils

This beautiful Georgian doorway, caught in sunlight, was drawn with Derwent watercolour pencils

CUTLERS' HALL
Church Street. Map reference 8

Opposite the Sheffield Cathedral you will find the Cutler's Hall, built in 1832 and extended in 1867. The ancient 'Company of Cutlers in Hallamshire' was founded in 1624, a Master Cutler is elected each year and acts as an ambassador for Sheffield and its industry. The annual Cutlers' Feast is a major occasion which takes place in the large Banqueting Hall with its Minstrels' Gallery. The interior of the building contains grandiose rooms and impressive collections of paintings and cutlery. Visits are by appointment only—so do make enquiries first.

Cutlers' Hall, Church Street (7 × 10) pencil, ink and wash

Some time ago, I spent two years at the Cutlers' Hall drawing the interior for a book publication Portraits of the Cutler's Hall. *During that time I got to know the staff there very well which made the task of drawing every room (understanding perspective is essential!) that much easier. Inside the building it is surprisingly quiet and one can hardly hear the noise from the busy street outside.*

*Standing with the Sheffield Cathedral behind me, I began by making a brief on the spot sketch. With Supertram sliding past, and temporarily blocking the view, it prompted me to take photographs of the building should I need to work from them later. This viewpoint was face on, so parallel perspective came into play here. Indoors, I drew out the sketch again onto smooth 140lb watercolour paper. I did not overwork the detail and suggested, rather than drew in, every line. I washed in Cobalt Blue for the sky, and for the rest of the painting I introduced the **variegated wash technique** by applying washes of Raw Sienna, Cobalt Blue, and Cadmium Red diagonally across the paper, allowing the colours to merge together while still wet. When dry, I painted over the dark areas, i.e. the windows and doorways, with a mix of Cobalt Blue and Cadmium Red. With pen and ink I highlighted the detail on the building and added some figures.*

- Pauline Shearstone -

INDUSTRIAL HERITAGE

KELHAM ISLAND MUSEUM
Alma Street, off Corporation Street. Map reference 9

With a mill race constructed alongside the River Don to power waterwheels in the 12th century, the Kelham Island area was created and became a busy industrial location. The building which houses the present museum was built in 1897 as a steam-powered electricity generating station for the Sheffield Tramways. I remember visiting the site in 1980, before it opened as a museum, and writing, 'industrial objects and machines fill the huge building waiting to be inspected, repaired or renovated...the clanking of hammers on steel and men busy working give the impression that there is still a lot of hard work to be done...'[1]

Today, Kelham Island Museum is a 'living museum' telling *The Story of Sheffield* with its *Mighty River Don Steam Engine* and specialised craftspeople working in a row of *Little Mesters* workshops built along a Victorian cobbled street. Visit *The Melting Shop* where children are 'processed like steel'[2] and explore *The Energy Zone* with its hands-on discovery area for children. The Museum has a shop and café too. All this and so much more—as the ad. might say!

'Made in Sheffield is a mark of quality...'[3] If you want to know about Sheffield's great industrial traditions and achievements then a visit here is must.

Telephone: 0114 272 2106

1. *Sheffield Sketches.* Pauline Shearstone, 1980.
2. & 3. *Kelham Island Museum.* Leaflet.

The River Don Steam Engine
(5 × 7) watercolour print

Built in 1905 by Davy Brothers, this 12,000 horse power engine once powered a huge rolling mill and is one of the most powerful surviving engines of its kind. It is usually in steam twice a day.

This picture was part of a much larger watercolour I painted showing the many aspects of Kelham Island Museum. I worked from several photographs which enabled me to paint the precise detail so necessary for this type of painting. Commissioned by Davy McKee (Sheffield) Limited, this watercolour was one of many of my paintings donated by companies to HMS Sheffield.

ABBEYDALE INDUSTRIAL HAMLET

Abbeydale Road South, opposite Ecclesall Woods

From the centre of Sheffield we journey along Abbeydale Road South to find a unique 18th-century collection of buildings, the Abbeydale Industrial Hamlet. Here, in a courtyard, are buildings where scythes and steel edge tools were once manufactured. Preserved is a Crucible Steel Furnace, 'the only one in the world'[1] which produced crucible steel invented by Benjamin Huntsman in 1742. Tilt hammers forged the ingots powered by an eighteen foot water-wheel, which also ran the grinding machinery. The dam, which stores the water to work the machinery, is now in the Beauchief Gardens reached further along the road. Of particular interest is the Manager's House, furnished in the style of the late Victorian period, and the row of workmen's cottages. Recently the hamlet was closed but has now been taken over by Sheffield Industrial Museums Trust who propose to open the Museum to the public again shortly, this is good news as the site is one of great industrial and historical importance.

(N.B. The summer of 1998 has seen the Hamlet being opened during the school holiday period.)

1. *The Sheffield Knife Book: A History and Collectors' Guide.* Geoffrey Tweedale, The Hallamshire Press, 1996.

Abbeydale Industrial Hamlet Sketchbook Page (9 × 7¹/₄) watercolour

It was very difficult to include just one illustration of the Hamlet. Having spent several years there as Artist-in-Residence, I have numerous paintings and sketches of the place and its craftspeople to choose from. The hamlet particularly came alive on Working Days when craftsmen worked at their various skills. Memories of Ron Staley, the Scythe Grinder, who swung precariously on a rope sling hanging from the ceiling; Stan Gregory, the Hand Forger, working in one of the old forges; Brian and Edgar the skilled Crucible team; and not forgetting the lovely aroma of freshly-baked bread from the black-leaded oven in the Manager's house. So tempting to eat and so delicious!

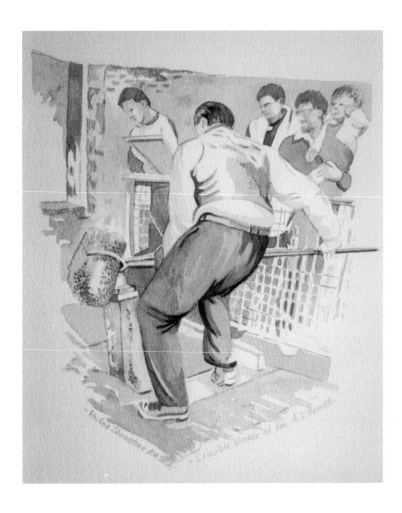

Edgar and Brian, the Crucible Team working at the Hamlet on Working Days
(Two watercolours taken from my sketchbook)

SHEPHERD WHEEL
Off Hangingwater Road, Sheffield 11

After our visit to Abbeydale Industrial Hamlet we arrive at Shepherd Wheel which is another water-powered complex. Situated on the west side of the city in Whiteley Woods, Shepherd Wheel stands on a most beautiful stretch of the River Porter.

This small grinding 'Wheel' was first recorded in 1584, being referred to then as 'Potar Whele'. The Wheel, however, takes its name from a Mr Shepherd who, in 1794, rented the property consisting of ten troughs (pronounced trows)...and 'employed ten grinders'. Water for the wheel was 'diverted from the river at Porter Bridge'.[1]

The large, cast-iron water-wheel, seen at the back of the building, powered the two workshops where the grinders (or Little Mesters as they were called in the cutlery trade) worked at their troughs. Grinding was a difficult job, with problems arising from the dust and injuries sustained when a grindstone burst. A local grinding song relates 'there's more than you'd imagine in the grinding of a blade...' which is evident on a visit here.

Until recently, Shepherd Wheel was a City Museum where schoolchildren and visitors could see for themselves this unique piece of Sheffield's Industrial past.

I have painted here many times. On cold days when the Museum was open, I was more than grateful for the warm fire inside. The attendant made the place come alive, with his historical knowledge and commentary, which made visits particularly interesting.

1. *Shepherd Wheel.* A Sheffield City Museums Publication, 1984.

Shepherd Wheel in Snow (6 × 8¹⁄₂) watercolour

One year I used this watercolour for my Christmas card.

I drew in a simple outline and painted in a subdued palette of Cobalt Blue and Indian Red which suggested the purple snow effect. To add a warm contrast, the building was painted with diluted Burnt Sienna.

CITY
SQUARES

~Pauline Shearstone. AYA. FRSA.~

CATHEDRAL SQUARE
Church Street. Map reference 10

Sheffield has several squares, and in this section we look at just three of them, starting with the most central one, Cathedral Square, named after the Cathedral Church of St Peter and St Paul. The earliest reference to the Sheffield Parish Church was in 1286, although no traces of a building of that date survive.

The present church was built in the 15th century with its modern extension, including fifty-feet-high columns, completed in 1966. *The Shrewsbury Chapel* contains memorials relating to the 4th and 6th Earls, while the *Chapel of St George* contains the ensign of *HMS Sheffield* and a screen of swords and bayonets. The stained glass window in the *Chapter House* depicts scenes from Sheffield's past. Outside, in the grounds, is the statue of *James Montgomery*, a poet, philanthropist and Editor of Sheffield's *Iris* newspaper.

Cathedral Square (11½ × 19) watercolour

Weekdays are busy here, so one Sunday morning I visited the Square to rough-out sketches and take photographs. I decided to leave out the Supertram but indicated its presence by including the rail track and sign! By using a mainly transparent palette of Raw Sienna, Burnt Sienna and Rose Madder, I managed to keep the painting looking fresh.

47

PARADISE SQUARE
Off Campo Lane. Map reference 11

From Cathedral Square to Paradise Square, a place of Georgian elegance and one of the most historic parts of the city. The area can be entered from Campo Lane, a little street behind the Cathedral.

This square was once a cornfield called, Hick's Stile Field. The houses on the east side were built in 1736 followed, in 1771, by further building which formed the square as it appears to this day. In the 18th century a market was held here where pots and pans were sold, this led to the square being called 'Pot Square'. The street lamps, brickwork patterns and street cobbles are reminders of Paradise Square in earlier days.

In 1779, John Wesley preached to his largest congregation on a weekday here. No. 18, once a Masonic hall, with a flight of steps leading up from the outside to a door on the first floor, made it an ideal place for preachers and orators.

At No. 24, Sir Francis Chantrey, the famous sculptor who was born at Norton, had his studio here as a portrait painter in 1802. Over at No. 12, David Daniel Davis, a physician who assisted at the birth of Queen Victoria, lived from 1803 until 1812.

During the week the square is busy with lawyers and solicitors at work. To soak in the Georgian atmosphere visit the square on a Sunday when a quietness allows one to sketch here without having too many reminders of modern-day life.

Paradise Square (7 × 17½) line & wash

The Square's steep incline, with the ornate buildings appearing to cling together for support, captured my imagination. This curve formed an important part of the drawing. I decided to use line and wash for this picture, so I began by working out my sketch onto a 140lb Bockingford NOT watercolour paper. When I was satisfied with this I worked over it with pen and ink adding a few simple colour washes beginning with Cerulean and Cobalt Blue for the sky and progressing to Raw Sienna for the foreground. A basic mix of Cobalt Blue and Light Red was used for the houses, while diluted Cobalt Blue was added to the windows and roofs. White areas were left to accentuate the steep sweep of the Square.

-Pauline Shearstone-

-Paradise Square-

TUDOR SQUARE
Off Norfolk Street. Map reference 12

Tudor Square, bordered by Norfolk and Surrey Streets, is a fairly new pedestrian area, an open space with a grassed oval, ideal for entertainment performances and a meeting place for locals and tourists alike. Perhaps it should be called Arts Square being surrounded as it is by The Crucible Theatre, renowned for its theatre productions and the World Snooker Championships, and The Lyceum, a superb grandiose theatre.

Nearby, is The Central Library with The Graves Art Gallery, named after its benefactor J.G. Graves, on the third floor. (There is a lift for those unable to climb the stairs.) The gallery displays British art from the 16th century to the present, European paintings and a collection of watercolours, prints and drawings. In one of the smaller galleries is The Grice Collection of Chinese Ivories which is permanently on show. The gallery's coffee bar serves light refreshments and displays small exhibitions.

Also part of the Square's complex is the Ruskin Gallery, St Marie's Cathedral, on Norfolk Row, completes the scene.

Tudor Square (8 × 12¾) watercolour

2 'L'
shapes

I consider designing a picture to be so important that I have included an entire section on composition later in the book. To help you choose the best composition for your painting take two L-shaped cards, which act as a viewfinder, and look through them as if you are going to take a photograph of the scene in front of you. Do not paint your picture in the same shape every time. Get into the habit of thinking in horizontal, vertical or panoramic shapes instead.

My Tudor Square sketch shows there is more than one viewpoint that I could have used for my painting.

To help you isolate a subject, try placing two L-shaped cards over your own sketches or photographs before you start a painting.

THE LYCEUM THEATRE
Tudor Square. Map reference 13

The Lyceum, standing alongside *The Crucible Theatre*, has had quite a chequered career. Opened in 1897 it set the trend for lavish musicals and the traditional family pantomime. In 1961 the theatre closed, although the panto continued until 1969. Plans for its demolition were announced in 1963 but were never brought to fruition. Bingo helped to keep it going in 1966 but in 1969 a 'Keep Lyceum Live' campaign was started. The theatre suffered another threat of demolition in 1972 but, in that year, the Hallamshire Historic Buildings Society, managed to get the Lyceum 'listed'. The Lyceum Theatre Trust, formed in 1975, planned to buy the building, renovate and re-open it.

After many years of being empty the Lyceum was finally resurrected to its former glory after a superb restoration and renovation programme. Following a determined effort by numerous people, the theatre finally opened its doors to the public once more in December, 1990. With its lavish interior and splendid Victorian facade, the Lyceum is now the jewel in Tudor Square's crown, housing top touring productions, including West End bound shows, the RSC, ballet and opera.

The Lyceum Theatre (9 × 10½) watercolour

I used a Winsor & Newton 140lb rough paper and worked out the composition first on some cartridge paper. My main interest was the tall corner window which I found attractive to paint. Using my sketch as a guide, I drew onto the watercolour paper gently with a 2B pencil, positioning the perspective lines and making sure that the building was sufficiently detailed before I started to paint. The drawing was of prime importance as it acted as a good foundation for the painting. I began by washing in Raw Sienna and French Ultramarine into the sky area. When dry, I painted an overall wash of Raw Sienna over the building, leaving some of the white paper showing through. The windows came next, using Light Red painted into the corner window and onto the front of the building. I introduced a diluted wash of Payne's Gray over the building and darkened the windows with Light Red and French Ultramarine. The mix for the foreground grass area was Raw Sienna and Payne's Gray with a darker green mix washed over later for the cast shadow. Certain areas were darkened with Payne's Gray to complete the painting.

ARTS
&
PARKS

WESTON PARK, CITY MUSEUM & MAPPIN ART GALLERY
Western Bank. Map references 14 & 15

WESTON PARK
The city's most central park being only a short distance from the Town Hall. Across the road from the Children's Hospital and overlooking the red brick buildings of the University of Sheffield, this park has seen better days but is still a good refuge from the city traffic. With the nearby boating lake and housing the City Museum and Mappin Art Gallery, it is a park enjoyed by families and art enthusiasts alike. The Museum and Art Gallery are part of the same building and both contain particularly interesting displays and exhibits.

THE CITY MUSEUM
After the park came into the possession of Sheffield Corporation, in 1873, Weston House, once the home of Eliza and Anne Harrison, opened in 1875 as the City Museum. Years later the accommodation was found to be inadequate and, in 1937, a new City Museum was opened. Various alterations have taken place since then in order to house the numerous exhibits, including the world's finest collection of Old Sheffield Plate.

Weston Park with Bandstand and Arts Tower (5 × 12) pencil and watercolour

The Arts Tower, standing 255 feet above ground level, dominates the park's skyline contrasting against the old bandstand, a reminder of the park's former glory days. This is a very loose picture, drawn out with a 2B pencil onto 140lb smooth watercolour paper. Flat washes of Alizarin Crimson for the trees, Cobalt Blue for the sky and Cadmium Yellow mixed with French Ultramarine for the grass and background trees, were painted in using a flat 1/2-inch brush.

-Pauline Shearstone-

THE MAPPIN ART GALLERY

Opened in 1887, the gallery came into existence through the direction of John Newton Mappin who bequeathed his collection of paintings to the city. After the opening of the Gallery a further donation of paintings was presented by his nephew, Sir Frederick Thorpe Mappin, who later gave more gifts thereby creating the beginning of the city's art collection. The Gallery has a permanent display of Victorian paintings, and stages shows from its own collections and major touring exhibitions. In recent years The Mappin has featured exhibitions which have included new media and work by contemporary artists. Art Workshops include print making, life drawing and children's classes which, together with the coffee bar, help to create an active atmosphere.

— City Museum & the Mappin Art Gallery —

City Museum and the Mappin Art Gallery (4 × 16) pen illustration

This fine building, built during 1886–88, features 'the Grecian Ionic style of architecture'.[1] A flight of steps leads you up into the portico flanked by giant Ionic colonnades. At the side of the gallery is the Memorial Column in memory of Godfrey Sykes. The long building dominates the park and in order to capture this effect a panoramic composition was chosen. The Museum on the left was drawn in a curve so that the huge colonnades would be the main feature. I worked out several sketches before choosing this final design and began by drawing an outline with an HB pencil. Ink was then introduced using an Artpen. For the darkest tones I added a solid black with a felt-tip pen to emphasise the tonal contrast between the dark and light areas.

1. *A Popular History of Sheffield.* J.E. Vickers.

ART GALLERY

— Pauline Shearstone —

BOTANICAL GARDENS
Clarkehouse Road. Map reference 16

The Botanical Gardens, a green oasis hidden away from the city traffic, is an ideal painting location. The gardens house floral displays and 'a national plant collection with more than 5,500 different plants'.[1] However, you do not have to be a flower painter to paint here as there are other subjects to paint too.

Opened in 1836, the gardens were a favourite place to promenade. A meeting place, where ladies in particular would promenade to the music of the band. The three glass conservatories were originally linked by glass corridors. Two of these conservatories once housed an aviary and an aquarium which were favourite attractions for children.

All manner of events have been staged here, from Blondin, the famous tightrope-walker, performing 'his daring feats above the tree tops'[2] to children watching the bears in the bear pit begging for buns. The pit still survives as a sad reminder of this earlier 'amusement'.

A recent award of five million pounds from the National Lottery, will allow the gardens to be restored to their former Victorian glory, along with the opening of a new café, shop and visitors' centre. Queen Victoria, whose statue towers above the flower beds, if not amused, would at least be pleased!

1. *Sheffield.* Sheffield Telegraph, 1998.
2. *A Popular History of Sheffield*, (p. 232). J. Edward Vickers. E.P. Publishing, 1978.

West Pavilion, Botanical Gardens ($7^{1}/_{2} \times 6^{1}/_{4}$) watercolour

It was a hot sunny day when I painted this watercolour. This particular Pavilion has special memories for me, for it was here that my students and I held our annual painting exhibition. It was an ideal setting and quite unlike a formal gallery atmosphere. Those who would not readily visit a gallery, found it easy to view the paintings here without any obligation. It was a most enjoyable way of introducing art to people.

I chose a 140lb Bockingford paper for my painting and limited my palette to a selection of greens, using Cadmium Yellow, Winsor Blue and Burnt Umber. For the sky I used a wash of Cerulean Blue and added the background trees with a blue-green mix. The brighter tree on the right had more Cadmium Yellow added to the green mix, while Rose Madder and French Ultramarine were added for the purple bush. Cadmium Yellow was washed over the foreground, superimposed with a darker green wash for the shadow. Raw Sienna was introduced to the building, while Rose Madder and French Ultramarine were used for the windows.

WHIRLOW BROOK PARK
Hathersage Road, Sheffield 11

Travelling out of the city along Ecclesall Road South we reach Whirlow Brook Park. Set well back away from the Hathersage Road, Whirlow Brook has some lovely walks surrounding it, leading from Limb Brook to Ringinglow. The house now accommodates conferences and functions as well as a café, but it was originally built as a private residence, around 1906, for Mr and Mrs Percy Fawcett. They remained here until 1920, when Mr Walter Benton Jones' family moved into Whirlow Brook. It was Mrs Benton Jones, a keen horticulturist, who sought the advice of The Royal Horticultural Society in the planning of the large grounds. She helped create, with the planting of the fine trees, shrubs, rock gardens and lakes, the gardens that we see today. In 1946 Whirlow Brook with its extensive grounds was purchased for £15,000 by The Town Trustees, the Graves Charitable Trust and Sheffield Corporation. In 1951 Whirlow Brook was opened to the public who have enjoyed, and continue to enjoy, one of the most beautiful areas of parkland belonging to the City of Sheffield.

1. & 2. See *Whirlow: The Story of an Ancient Sheffield Hamlet.* Shirley Frost, 1990.

Whirlow Brook Park ($8^{1}/_{2} \times 6^{3}/_{4}$) watercolour

BEAUCHIEF ABBEY
Beauchief Drive, off Abbey Lane

A short distance from Whirlow is Beauchief, where the 12th-century Abbey nestles below the headland of trees. This is the last painting on my city journey. From here we take the road out to The Peak District, where we prepare to meet a new challenge—the art of landscape painting.

JOURNEY INTO THE PEAK

THE PEAK DISTRICT

People who live in Sheffield are so fortunate to have the area known as The Peak District within such a short distance of the City. Established in 1951 and 'covering 542 square miles'.[1] The Peak was Britain's first National Park.

There were settlements here as long ago as the Iron Age and every care is taken for the conservation of 'the landscape and the provision of facilities for visitors'[2] while at the same time making sure that the interests of local people are not forgotten. The Old English word 'peac' (meaning hill) gives its name to the area.

The Peak District consists of two areas, in the central and southern parts is the 'White Peak' formed of limestone millions of years ago. It is much gentler than its northern counterpart the 'Dark Peak' with its craggy moorland, good for climbers and mountain sheep, and formed of millstone grit or 'gritstone'. Abandoned millstones, once made to sharpen steel or to grind corn, are evidence of earlier industries.

The Peak District is an area of contrast. The villages in the White Peak are to be found where they are protected from the winter winds and are built around the village pond close to the water supply. In the Dark Peak, villages are usually found in sheltered river valleys and are more isolated.

With so much to offer in natural and outstanding beauty, it is not surprising that The Peak District is such a favourite place to visit time and time again.

1. & 2. *See Look at the Peak National Park.* Bessacarr Prints, 1986.

Composition is the creation of balanced shapes within a picture which guide the viewer in to the main feature or focal point. Good composition is when a shape that is pleasing to the eye is created. Using a viewfinder or two L-shapes is helpful (see Project Page 51).

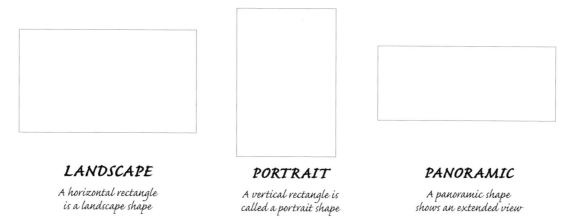

LANDSCAPE
A horizontal rectangle is a landscape shape

PORTRAIT
A vertical rectangle is called a portrait shape

PANORAMIC
A panoramic shape shows an extended view

GOOD COMPOSITIONAL SHAPES
Shapes that are pleasing to the eye

The L-shape *The triangle* *The Z-shape*

Think in thirds

✔ Good

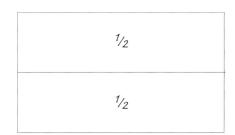

Not the Union Jack

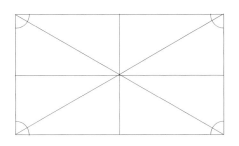

✘ Bad

DON'T cut into two equal parts by placing the focal point in the centre

Two equals are not pleasing to the eye

When painting a landscape consider the three elements that a landscape contains i.e. the sky, trees and the foreground. The sky plays an important role in a painting, so here are two skies for you to practise by applying paint onto a wet surface. This technique is called 'wet-into-wet'.

A WET-INTO-WET SKY

1. Make sure your board is sloping to allow the paint to run down the paper.

2. Wet the sky area only.

3. While still damp, apply Raw Sienna diagonally across the sky.

4. Run in French Ultramarine into the damp paper taking care not to work the blue into the yellow—otherwise you will create a green sky!

4. With a mix of French Ultramarine and Burnt Umber add a simple foreground to complete your landscape.

A SUNNY SKY WITH CLOUDS

1. Wet the paper and while damp apply *Raw Sienna* across the sky.

2. Using *French Ultramarine* paint in between the clouds. Don't paint the actual clouds, but the area between them which is called the negative area.

3. While still damp, drop in a mix of *Payne's Gray* and *Rose Madder* (or *Alizarin Crimson*) and paint the underneath of the clouds. Leave the top edges of the clouds light by allowing the white paper and the *Raw Sienna* to show through.

Sky Hints

- The sky is usually darker at the top and becomes paler as it reaches the horizon.

- To create perspective in a sky, streaks of paint become narrower and closer together as the sky meets the horizon.

- When painting a wet-into-wet sky try not to flood the paper with too much water as, the more water you use, the less control you have.

- Using too much water results in a pale watercolour. When the water dries out you are left with a weak amount of paint showing.

- Practise painting and sketching skies outdoors as much as time allows.

Constable, a great landscape painter, sketched extensively outdoors and captured many sky variations. 'Skies were to become one of the major preoccupations of his mature work.'[1]

1. *Constable by John Sutherland.* Encyclopaedia Britannica, Vol. II, (p.8).

Trees are such main features in a landscape that being able to paint a tree convincingly is very important. Take your sketchbook outdoors and learn to understand the anatomy of a tree by trying to draw one. Every tree has its own familiar shape. The oak is sturdy and dense while the silver birch is tall and elegant. A winter tree reveals its branches while the summer tree is covered in a thick foliage of varying greens. Siennas and umbers are seen in autumn. All these factors create a challenge to the artist. Practise drawing a tree first before attempting to paint one.

DRAWING A TREE

1. Draw the outline of the tree. See its overall shape first

2. Introduce the main branches

3. Draw in the foliage. Keep to the main outline shape

✔ ✘

Branches grow out of the main trunk like this   Not this

PAINTING TREES

1. Painting one side lighter than the other creates the form of the tree.
2. To suggest foliage use a fairly thick mix and work with the side of your brush.
3. Using rough watercolour paper helps give texture to trees.

1. Basic wash of Cadmium Yellow + Winsor Blue. (More yellow in the mix)

2. Next wash (while still wet) Cadmium Yellow + Winsor Blue + Burnt Umber

3. Final darker mix of Burnt Umber + Winsor Blue. Branches — scrape out with finger nail

Foregrounds should relate to the painting and not be just a frieze along the bottom of your picture. Most beginners tend to find foregrounds difficult and leave this part of the painting until last in the vain hope that everything will be alright! Try not to overwork a foreground. Sometimes, a simple foreground with just a shadow cast across it, is quite adequate. Here are few helpful guidelines:

TEXTURAL FOREGROUND EFFECTS

1. Splatter paint onto the foreground using an old toothbrush.

2. Scraping out with your fingernail while the paint is still wet helps suggest grass.

3. Wet-into-wet. Wet the paper first before running in different colours.

4. Wax your foreground (with a piece of candle) before applying your paint. The wax resists the paint and remains white. This technique is especially useful for adding texture to stone walls.

5. Apply Masking Fluid to the area where you want it to be kept white. Use an old paintbrush and, when dry, paint over the masked-out area. Rub off the masking fluid with your fingers, then either paint over the white area or leave white.

6. Overlaying washes. This is a simple technique of applying a darker wash over a lighter one. The technique can be used to create shadow effects which are particularly useful for suggesting depth in foregrounds.

EXPERIMENT with the above techniques before using them in a painting. Try not to use too many different techniques in one painting as the overall effect then looks too gimmicky!

1. *SPLATTER*

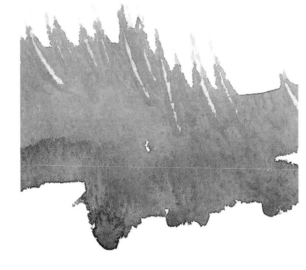

2. *SCRAPING OUT*

3. *WET-INTO-WET*

4. *WAX*

5. *MASKING FLUID*

6. *OVERLAYING WASHES*

THE PEAK DISTRICT

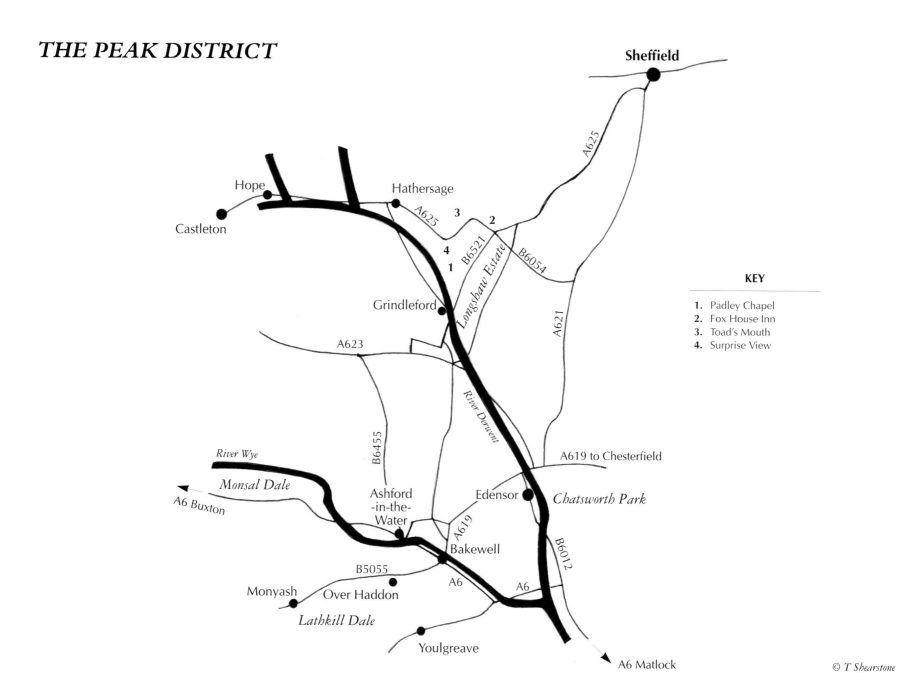

Sheffield

Hope

Castleton

Hathersage

A625

A625

3

2

4

B6521

1

B6054

Longshaw Estate

A621

Grindleford

A623

River Derwent

B6455

A619 to Chesterfield

River Wye

Monsal Dale

Ashford -in-the- Water

Edensor

Chatsworth Park

A6 Buxton

A619

Bakewell

B6012

B5055

Monyash

Over Haddon

A6

A6

Lathkill Dale

Youlgreave

A6 Matlock

KEY

1. Padley Chapel
2. Fox House Inn
3. Toad's Mouth
4. Surprise View

© T Shearstone

PADLEY
TO
CASTLETON

PADLEY CHAPEL
Off the B6521, near Grindleford. Map reference 1

Our journey into The Peak District starts at Padley which you can reach either by following the path down from Longshaw, through Padley Wood and on into Padley, or by walking from Grindleford Railway Station and continuing along the rough track until you reach Padley Chapel.

Padley Chapel was once a part of Padley Hall, built in about 1400 by the Padley family. Later it came to be owned by the Fitzherbert family who were devout Catholics. In Elizabeth I's reign, Catholics were liable to prison sentences and death for practising their religion. Priests celebrating Mass had to do so in secret, so this little chapel, which was on the upper floor of the gatehouse of the Hall, was hidden from view.

John Fitzherbert's eldest son, Thomas, wished to inherit his father's estate so he plotted with Richard Topcliffe, who was a professional priest-catcher, and the Earl of Shrewsbury, and informed on his father when he was at Padley. Acting on information given by Thomas, the Earl made a surprise visit to Padley and captured Fitzherbert together with two Catholic priests, Nicholas Garlick and Robert Ludlam, who were found hiding in a chimney. They were arrested on July 12th, 1588.

Days later the two priests, together with another priest, Richard Sympson, were, 'hung drawn and quartered in Derby'.[1] Fitzherbert's life was spared by a £10,000 security paid by his son-in-law, but was sent to prison and died there ten years later. Thomas initially received his inheritance but only for a while as, after a legal wrangle, he lost it to Richard Topcliffe who then lived at Padley Hall. After Elizabeth I's death it reverted back to the Fitzherbert family once more.

1. *Historical Buildings of Derbyshire.* John Merrill.
Also *Look at Padley.* Bessacarr Prints 1988.

The Hall eventually became a farm, with the surviving chapel being used as a barn. In 1933, restoration work was begun. The chapel's stained glass windows tell its history, and the priests, who suffered such a terrible fate, are remembered each year by a pilgrimage which takes place at Padley on the Sunday closest to the 12th July.

Padley Chapel (6 × 5) pen & ink

Drawn on a smooth watercolour paper this pen drawing highlighted my fascination with the building's unusual stonework. The many variations of texture and line work required for this drawing suited the dexterity of the Artpen so well.

Padley Chapel (9 × 7) watercolour & watercolour pencils

This watercolour was inspired after seeing Padley Chapel on a cold, misty day which made it seem quite eerie. I chose a limited palette of blues and greys to suggest this hazy, misty atmosphere.

An overall wash set the tone for this picture. Working on a 140lb Winsor & Newton rough watercolour paper I washed over the dry paper with Cobalt Blue, Raw Sienna and Rose Madder. While the paper was still wet, I highlighted the chapel by adding more Raw Sienna.

With a mix of Cobalt Blue and Raw Sienna, I painted in the background trees, while a drybrush technique (use less water) was applied for the foreground tree, using a mix of Cobalt Blue and a little Raw Sienna. Raw Sienna, Burnt Umber and Cobalt Blue were painted into the foreground taking care to leave some of the first overall wash showing through. The shadow colour on the chapel and the windows was a warm mix of Cobalt Blue and Rose Madder.

For final details I introduced blue, yellow and red watercolour pencils dry, to highlight colours in the windows and on the chapel wall.

Longshaw Lodge (12 × 4) pencil

Built as a shooting lodge, over 160 years ago, by the 6th Duke of Rutland to accommodate himself and his friends at grouse shooting times, this fine building had its own chapel, stables and servant's rooms. It is a striking feature of Longshaw and makes an excellent subject for drawing.

Although I had originally intended this picture to be a rough sketch, I became more interested in the tonal contrast that the picture created and so developed it further into a detailed drawing. The dark tones of the background trees were emphasised to contrast against the lighter tones of the building. The loose treatment in the foreground was deliberately left unfinished to lead the eye into the picture.

LONGSHAW ESTATE
Between Fox House and Grindleford by the B6521

From Padley Chapel, walk up through Padley Woods, an ancient woodland. Cross the road and journey on past a pond which now serves as home for dragonflies and frogs but where once, in earlier days, stood a boat house and a pier for swimmers. This vast area of moorland, woods and farmland is Longshaw, some 1500 acres in total, and situated less than eight miles away from the City of Sheffield.

Longshaw Estate (6¹/₂ × 13) watercolour

Longshaw has many moods. One August I was giving a painting demonstration here to a group of visitors from abroad when we heard a rumbling noise in the distance. 'It's nothing to worry about' I said and continued to paint. But the sky became increasingly darker until a loud crack of thunder signalled the end of the demonstration. 'I think we'd better shelter before the rain starts' I suggested, turning round to find the entire group running in the direction of the café! After a short while, and many coffees later, the sun began to shine as if the storm had never existed. 'Gee, Pauline' one American lady exclaimed 'how do you manage to control the weather!'

Fox House Inn (8 × 12) watercolour pencil and ink

A gentle sepia sketch drawn on a smooth 140lb watercolour paper using a brown (Copper Beech) watercolour pencil.
To emphasise the dark branches of the trees, sepia ink was applied with a dip pen.

FOX HOUSE INN
On the A625. Map reference 2

Just across from the Longshaw Estate, situated on the Sheffield Road, is the Fox House Inn, a popular place especially with hikers. It was here, supposedly, that two local farmers who had been boasting about their sheepdogs, decided to hold a competition to see who had the better dog. The trial, held in the meadow at Longshaw, resulted in the Sheepdog Trials which are now held here each September.

- Toad's Mouth -

- Pauline Shearstone -

TOAD'S MOUTH
By the A625. Map reference 3

From the Fox House Inn the road continues on towards Hathersage. Here, on the bend of the road, is an unusually shaped rock which is affectionately known in the area as Toad's Mouth.

Old grindstones, scattered around the moorland here, are reminders of days when the local stone provided Sheffield with its grinding wheels for the water mills and workshops.

The area is renowned for its walks and its rugged beauty.

Mist over the Surprise. Drawing from my sketchbook

THE SURPRISE

The mist in the valley for the painting, *The Surprise* was painted using a technique called 'lifting out'.

This method creates a soft edge instead of a crisp one. While the colour is still wet carefully remove the colour, using a dry brush, a tissue, or even a cotton bud. This technique can be used to soften the edges of clouds or to paint a simple sky (see A Simple Sky Wash p. 19). Make sure that you, 'dab and lift' rather than damage the surface of your paper by rubbing out.

Certain colours stain the paper (e.g. Alizarin Crimson) and are, therefore, not the best to use with this technique. If you are not sure which colours stain, test them first to see if you can remove them off the paper.

Not only is this technique good to soften edges and create a misty effect but it can also be used to create highlights. Masking fluid can reserve a white area for you and adding Chinese White or white gouache can suggest highlights, but the brightest or whitest highlight will always be the white of the paper.

Mist over the Surprise ($6^{1}/_{2} \times 12^{1}/_{2}$) watercolour

THE SURPRISE
On the A625. Map reference 4

The Surprise, so called for, on reaching it, one is suddenly confronted with one of the most marvellous views of the area. Here, Hathersage and the Hope Valley are spread out before you. It is hard to imagine that the City of Sheffield is only a few miles away.

HATHERSAGE
On the A625,
see map page 70

The road down from the Surprise takes you through Hathersage. It is hard to believe now, in this lovely setting, that in the 1800s a needle industry thrived here. Above the village, high on the hillside, stands the 14th-century Church of St Michael. Charlotte Brontë stayed at the vicarage here and named her heroine, Jane Eyre, from the Eyre family whose brasses can be seen in the church. Climb up the hill and visit the churchyard. Here is, reputedly, Little John's grave, measuring some 3.5 metres in length. For many years a large bow, arrows and a green cap were kept inside the church. Take time to explore Hathersage for there is much to see and plenty of good walks to enjoy.

HOPE
On the A625, see map page 70

From Hathersage, the road leads to Hope which gives its name to the Hope Valley. Stop here and wander around this village before journeying on towards Castleton. For walkers, The Pennine Way is just a short distance away in Edale. Hope Show is held over the August Bank Holiday, and the annual Well Dressing, or 'Well Flowering' as it was once called, still attracts many visitors to the village each year.

St Peter's Church, Hope (6 × 10¼) watercolour

Complete with its gargoyles and broad spire, the church is mainly 14th century and stands in the centre of the village on a sharp bend on the Castleton road.

Several thumbnail sketches helped me find the best composition. To these I added colour notes. Working on a 140lb Bockingford NOT paper, and using a ½-inch brush, I painted over my basic drawing. Clouds were darkening in the distance over Lose Hill so, to capture this sombre atmosphere, I wet the sky area and ran in a wash of Raw Sienna across the paper. I followed with French Ultramarine and Burnt Umber which were applied to the top of the paper and caused the sky to granulate. For the cool, distant hills I used a mix of Light Red and French Ultramarine and added more Light Red to the mix when painting the trees and gravestones. The church and surrounding wall was a mix of Burnt Umber and Raw Sienna. This painting was simple in its composition and choice of palette.

- Pauline Shearstone

CASTLETON
On the A625, see map page 70

A short drive away from Hope is Castleton, named after the Castle which was built by the son of William the Conqueror, Sir William Peveril. This Norman fortress is a reminder of the Normans' intent to keep control of the lead mining and hunting in the area.

The Keep was rebuilt in 1176, and from its high vantage point it commands an impressive view overlooking the village below. With Sir Walter Scott's tale Peveril of the Peak the Castle was immortalised in print.

Castleton, with its stone-built cottages and village green, is famous for many things. It is famous for its jewellery, made from Blue John stone, a fluorspar with coloured bands of deep purple, blue and white. Some suggest that its name came from the French 'Bleu Jaune' pertaining to the stone's colours.

Castleton is famous too for its caverns. At the head of a limestone gorge below Peveril Castle is Peak Cavern with its huge, arched entrance which once housed ropemaker's cottages. The cavern's passages lead deep into the hillside linking numerous caves with strange sounding names such as Devil's Cellar, Orchestra Chamber and Great Tom of Lincoln.

Speedwell Cavern takes its name from the coaching inn which once stood there. ' "All Speed" travellers were wished as they set off up the steep, winding and dangerous Winnats Pass.'[1] Here visitors are taken by boat to the Bottomless Pit along the Cavern's canal which was made by the miners to carry lead ore to the entrance. Boatmen had to push with their hands and feet against the roof to power their boat along.

The most colourful and best stalactites in Britain can be seen in Treak Cliff Cavern, while the famous spar of the Blue John Cavern, a lovely product of the limestone, was probably worked by the Romans.

From the wild gorge of Winnats Pass (Wind Gates) on up to the heights of Mam Tor, or the Shivering Mountain as it is often called due to its layers of crumbling shale and gritstone which cause land slips. At the top, nearly 1,700 feet above sea-level, is a most marvellous panoramic view of Hope Valley.

With such a wealth of caves, old mines and history, Castleton, set in the heart of the Peak, attracts many visitors each year.

1. *Castleton leaflet.* Bessacarr Prints, 1986.

Castleton from Goosehill Bridge (11 × 8) watercolour

Choose your time and day to paint in Castleton. Its popularity makes it a little difficult for the painter. I have taken painting groups here on many occasions but have tried to keep away from the main busy areas.

However, for the purpose of this book I chose to paint this popular view of Castleton. Taken from Goosehill Bridge it is a familiar route to Peak Cavern. Using my drawing and photograph I worked on the painting later in the studio.

It was the height of summer and everything seemed to be predominately green. To convey this atmosphere I began by painting an overall wash of green using Cobalt Blue and a little Raw Sienna. This wash created a feeling of gentleness and warmth.

More blue was added to the background and more yellow-green into the foreground. Washes tend to dry lighter so a darker green mix, of French Ultramarine and Cadmium Yellow, was added next. I had applied masking fluid first over the windows and chimneys to keep those areas white. A mix of Burnt Sienna was used on the cottages and walls while Cadmium Red with French Ultramarine was introduced into the water. With my fingers, I rubbed off the masking fluid to reveal the white paper which I left as highlights. The figures were added to give the picture life.

CASTLETON SKYLINE (5³/₄ × 11¹/₄) wax, watercolour and ink

It was late winter when I sketched Peveril Castle silhouetted against the warm sky. The twisting trees seemed to lean in towards the castle in quite an eerie way. Watercolour mixes very well with other media and in order to suggest the texture of the cliffs, I used a combination of watercolour, wax and black ink.

MATERIALS
Smooth (HP) 140lb watercolour paper
Small piece of candle wax
Black ink and a dip pen
Watercolours

METHOD
The sky outline was drawn in first before I rubbed candle wax over the rocky areas which were to be painted later. Take care not to overdo the wax as it is difficult (if not impossible) to remove later.

With a ¹/₂-inch flat brush, I washed in the sky diagonally across the paper with bands of *Cobalt Blue*, *Raw Sienna* and *Cadmium Red*. When dry, I drew in the trees with a broad nib and black acrylic ink. I allowed the ink to dry before painting over the wax (the cliffs) with a mix of *Cadmium Yellow* and *Cobalt Blue*. A warm grey of *Cadmium Red* and *French Ultramarine* was added for the castle and darker tones.

ASSIGNMENT
To suggest texture, or to add variety to a foreground, try using mixed media in your painting.
(See Foreground Techniques p. 68)

CHATSWORTH
TO
YOULGREAVE

CHATSWORTH
B6012, see map page 70

Chatsworth is one of the most popular places in the Peak District. Set on a slope above the River Derwent it commands extensive views of the beautiful deer park with its gently rolling hills and woodland. It is an ideal setting for this majestic mansion which is the home of the Duke and Duchess of Devonshire. Great artists and craftsmen have been called in throughout the years to 'decorate' Chatsworth, hence its profusion of grandeur both inside and out, earning Chatsworth its worthy title of *The Palace of the Peak*. As they say in Derbyshire 'All roads lead to Chatsworth'.

Whatever your reason for visiting Chatsworth, whether it is to tour the house, wander through the gardens, explore the farmyard or simply enjoy a typically English cup of tea and other refreshments in the Carriage House Restaurant, there is no grander setting than here.

That marvellous visionary, Capability Brown, laid out the deer park, together with the cascades and terraces. Another 'creator' of Chatsworth, Sir Joseph Paxton, who started here as a labourer's lad, fulfilled his boyhood ambition to re-model Chatsworth's grounds and created a great conservatory (since demolished) which served as a model for his Crystal Palace Exhibition of 1851.

Chatsworth can be overwhelming as there are so many subjects to paint here. At such a busy tourist attraction, consider the best place to draw without attracting too much attention to yourself. I have painted many times at Chatsworth without being unduly disturbed by onlookers.

The Rose Garden at Chatsworth...where everything seemed to merge into blobs of colour creating an 'impression' of the many roses there.
(8³/₄ × 12¹/₄) watercolour

When you go out to paint, try to forget what objects you have in front of you, a tree, a field...merely think, here is a little square of blue, here is an oblong of pink, here is a streak of yellow, and paint it just as it looks to you, the exact colour and shape, until it gives your own naive impression of the scene.
Claude Monet 1840–1926

I was interested in painting a panoramic view of Chatsworth which would show this long, ornate building surrounded by its distant hills. To find this view I had to walk up the grassy slope away from the house and look down on Chatsworth. Here was this long view which suggested the grandeur of Chatsworth. I made sketches first, using my Aquarelle pencil (soft), with sufficient detail added so that I could refer to them later. My final sketch, shown here, was extended by taping on an extra sheet of paper so that I could continue my drawing. Turner made additions in the same manner—so we are in good company!

PAINTING METHOD

Always plan your paintings before you start and make several sketches and colour notes when painting outdoors. Begin by drawing out your picture with a 2B pencil, try not to rub out too much as it will destroy the surface of your watercolour paper.

Paper   260lb rough watercolour paper

Palette   *Cerulean Blue, Cobalt Blue, Raw Sienna, Rose Madder, French Ultramarine, Burnt Umber, Cadmium Yellow, Burnt Sienna, Cadmium Red* and *Winsor Blue* (red shade)

— Chatsworth —

The sky

I wet the sky area using plenty of water and washed in *Cerulean Blue* and *Cobalt Blue* to the top of the sky with a No. 10 brush. Then I added *Raw Sienna* and a slight touch of *Rose Madder* to the bottom of the sky taking care to leave some white areas. I continued this sky wash over the distant hills so the sky and the horizon would merge. Skies are usually darker at the top and paler at the bottom. While the sky was still wet, I introduced two granulating colours, of *French Ultramarine* and *Burnt Umber*, to the top of the sky.

The distant hills and background

With the sky dry, I washed in a mix of *Cobalt Blue* and Light Red onto the distant hills. The trees were a mix of *Cobalt Blue* and *Cadmium Yellow*, with more blue than yellow added. Avoid painting distant hills green if you wish to add depth to your painting. It is all to do with aerial perspective, objects in the distance are paler in tone and bluer, so by adding blue to distant hills you create an illusion of depth in your landscapes.

The House

To suggest sunlight, I decided to leave part of the house white. I tend not to use white gouache in a painting, preferring to keep to the traditional watercolour method of leaving white paper showing. Planning your picture helps you to decide where to leave white areas in advance. With a No. 8 round brush, I painted in Raw Sienna onto the building and, while it was still wet, I added Burnt Umber. I allowed this to dry before a mix of Burnt Umber and Winsor Blue was added to the windows. With a tissue I dabbed off some of the strong colour. Varying the dark window shapes prevents the windows from looking like dominoes!

Trees and foreground

For the line of trees in front of the house, and the larger tree on the right, I used a basic mix of Cadmium Yellow and Winsor Blue adding Burnt Umber to make a darker green. For the suggestion of the trees' foliage, I painted on the side of my No. 8 brush. With my finger nail I scraped out suggestions of branches.

Using a ½-inch one-stroke brush, I washed in the foreground with Winsor Blue and Cadmium Yellow. I allowed it to dry before adding a further, darker, mix of Winsor Blue, Cadmium Yellow and Burnt Umber. While the paper was still wet, I dragged out a suggestion of grasses with my paintbrush handle.

Shadows and final details

Shadows were introduced onto the building, windows and pathway with a mix of Cobalt Blue and Light Red. Finally, to add life to the painting, I introduced some figures into the picture.

Chatsworth (7½ × 18½) watercolour

-Pauline Shearstone-

EDENSOR
On B6012 through Chatsworth Park

Inside Chatsworth Park is the village of Edensor (pronounced Ensor) which was 'removed from its original to its present site between 1838 and 1842'.[1] The sixth Duke of Devonshire, wishing to have it out of sight of Chatsworth, gave the task of creating this new village to Joseph Paxton who was later joined, in 1840, by John Robertson, a draughtsman to J.C. Loudon.

These fanciful buildings, with their Tudor chimneys, chalet-type roofs and Jacobean gables, create a most picturesque if somewhat artificial atmosphere.

The dominating church with its large spire came later in 1867. In its graveyard are memorials to Joseph Paxton and President Kennedy's sister.

1. *The Buildings of England: Derbyshire.* Nikolaus Pevsner, Penguin Books, 1979.

House at Edensor (6½ × 5½) line and wash

Edensor contains various architectural styles as this house shows. It is relatively easy to sit and sketch here as, apart from the usual group of pleasant walkers passing through the village, one can work comparatively undisturbed.

The composition was not a problem as I intended the house to be the focal point, with the wall and road leading into the centre of the picture.

It was a warm day so I could sit and draw in comfort. I began by drawing with a 2B pencil onto a smooth 140lb watercolour paper before applying four flat washes of:

1. *Cobalt Blue for the sky and background.*
2. *Raw Sienna with Burnt Umber for the building.*
3. *Cobalt Blue and Raw Sienna for the grass*
4. *Light Red with Cobalt Blue for the road.*

When the painting was dry I sketched over some areas of the painting with my Artpen.

Buxton Lodge (5 × 10¹/₂) pencil and wash

Outside Edensor village, near the entrance to Chatsworth Park, is this half-timbered building with brick infillings 'a design of Wyatville dated 1837'[1] and completed by Paxton in 1839.

I applied the same method as in the previous Edensor illustration but every precise detail is not included as, on this particular occasion, it was all I could manage to draw whilst sinking into wet, soggy grass!

1. *The Buildings of England: Derbyshire.* Nikolaus Pevsner, Penguin Books, 1979.

MONYASH
On the B5055 through Bakewell

The road to Monyash twists, turns and climbs steeply, bordered by endless limestone walls and green fields before the road dips to reveal the village, its church almost hidden by the trees in the distance.

Monyash was once the centre of the lead mining industry and a busy market town. Today it is a meeting place for hikers and tourists who can rest first, with a pint of tea at The Old Smithy Tea Rooms overlooking the village green, or, take coffee at The Village Store & Tea Room in Church Street, or have a stronger beverage at the Bull's Head Inn, before journeying on down into the beautiful Lathkill Dale.

Try to take the time to stop at Monyash, for it offers not only a place to rest but contains a wealth of subjects for the artist too.

John Gratton, the famous Quaker, lived in Monyash, a once-strong Quaker community. The ancient Church of St Leonard contains some interesting items, one of which is a very long, rather worm-eaten chest with bands of wrought iron encasing it. In the olden days, this old chest had three locks and three keys, one held by the vicar and the other two by his churchwardens, all of whom had to be present before the chest could be unlocked. Writing forty years ago, one author did discover the secret of the chest 'a black cassock with ruff attached and a sheet or two of brown paper'![1]

The church has a memorial to Thomas Cheney, a descendant of John Cheney who was 'struck down by Richard III' (who would have given his kingdom for a horse) 'at Bosworth field and left for dead.'[2] When Cheney's helmet was broken in the battle, he managed to cover his head with a bullock's scalp which lay nearby. It is from this incident that the Cheney's crest of a bull's scalp was derived.

1. *The Derbyshire Dales.* Norman Price.
2. *The King's England: Derbyshire.* Arthur Mee.

Monyash (5 × 11) pencil drawing

A page from my sketchbook

I drew this sketch while sitting near the pond. I have painted Monyash from this spot and it makes a good subject with the pond in the foreground and the church in the distance.

With my sketch as a guide, try painting this scene for yourself.

OVER HADDON
Off the B5055, south-west of Bakewell

A short distance from Monyash is Over Haddon, a little upland village with old stone houses, corners and alleyways, surrounded by fields with grey, stone walls. Like Monyash, this too was once a lead mining community. This Peakland village overlooks beautiful Lathkill Dale making it a popular place for visitors, especially at weekends, the craft centre and tea rooms are added attractions. From the top of Over Haddon one can look across the valley and see the 15th-century tower of Youlgreave Church in the distance.

LATHKILL DALE
Between Monyash, Youlgreave and Over Haddon

The River Lathkill, mentioned in Izaac Walton's The Compleat Angler in 1676, was described by Charles Cotton as 'the purest, the most transparent stream that I ever yet saw...and breeds the best Trouts in England'.[1] Trout swim in the pools near the mediaeval Conskbury Bridge far below the village.

From the bottom car park at Over Haddon, follow the steep, twisting road down to the river below. Descending is easy, the return journey can be strenuous, especially on a hot sunny day. Looking upward from the path, one can see the village dwarfed by the grandeur of Lathkill Dale's scenery with its massive rock formations and thick foliage—it is well worth the journey.

1. *Lathkill Dale.* Booklet.

St Anne's Church, Over Haddon
($8 \times 6^{1}/_{2}$) pen & ink

Tucked away from the pathway which leads down into Lathkill Dale, is this ornate building. Standing at the top of the village, the church looks over the fields beyond and from here one can see a storm coming well before it arrives in Over Haddon!

It was a rainy day when I attempted this drawing and, after spending most of the time sheltering in the church porch, I decided to take several photographs before going home, which I could work from later. (You just have to know when to quit!)

Using a smooth watercolour paper, I drew in the detail with a medium Aquarelle pencil. I then added water over the pencil work to suggest tone, finishing with an Artpen for the final details. Do resist the temptation to draw in every brick!

-Pauline Shearstone-

99

Autumn in Lathkill Dale (5¼ × 8) watercolour & ink

Autumn is a beautiful time of the year, rich in browns and oranges. A palette of Burnt Sienna, Burnt Umber and Cadmium Orange, were the main colours used for this painting.

YOULGREAVE
Between the A515 and B5056

From Over Haddon follow the winding road to Youlgreave which lies between the valleys of the Lathkill and Bradford rivers and, 'looks out to the ancient stone circles of Stanton Moor and Harthill Moor'.[1] Arbor Low, a most important stone circle, is only three miles away. Youlgreave is a most interesting place to visit with plenty of subjects to draw and paint, especially *All Saints Church* which one of the most impressive churches in The Peak District.

The church's east window, by Burne-Jones and William Morris, is a fine example of beautiful stained glass. Set in brilliant colours of orange, yellow, silver and gold, it depicts Christ blessing the world together with the four Evangelists.

The Norman font is very unusual, with a strange animal carved upside down and holding onto a tiny bowl. I spent some time wandering around the church and made several sketches, one of which has been developed into a **Painting Project** shown in the following pages.

Youlgreave still continues its Well Dressing tradition held each year at the end of June. This ancient custom may have started during the Black Death, 'as a thanksgiving for survivors escaping the plague through the purity of the waters'.[2]

1. *Derbyshire.* A Mee. Hodder & Stoughton, 1974.
2. *A Journey through The Peak District.*

YOULGREAVE

My sketch of Youlgreave Church was drawn in winter. The sun was shining which cast a shadow across the building.

The trees and tombstones surrounded the church almost hiding it from view. Later, when developing the painting, I emphasised this effect by making the trees dominant and adding a soft shadow onto the wall and across the foreground. Shadows are important in a painting as they give depth to a picture.

With my sketch as a guide, I drew in the outline of the church and trees with a 2B pencil onto a NOT surface, 200lb Bockingford watercolour paper.

To keep this painting fairly simple, I limited my palette to just a few colours. *French Ultramarine* was washed over the sky followed by a touch of *Raw Sienn*a.

Raw Sienna was my basic colour for the church adding later a mix of *Cobalt Blue* and Light Red for the shadows. My greens for the tree on the right, were *Winsor Blue* and *Burnt Umber* with a slight touch of *Raw Sienna*. For the rather stark tree on the left, I used *Raw Sienna* and *Payne's Gray*. A diluted mix of *Raw Sienna* and *Payne's Gray* was washed over the foreground grass. Here areas of white paper were left to suggest sunlight.

Placing your darkest tone against your lightest one helps to emphasise the focal point in your painting. As I had said all I wanted to say about this subject I left it well alone, resisting the temptation to paint in every minute detail. You have to know when to stop!

Youlgreave Church
Rough sketch and finished watercolour

ASHFORD
-IN-THE-
WATER
TO
BAKEWELL

ASHFORD-IN-THE-WATER
At the junction of the A6020 and the A6

The last part of our journey takes us from Ashford-in-the-Water, through Monsal Dale and down into Bakewell. These places are all very popular tourist attractions.

Ashford-in-the-Water, mentioned in the Domesday Book as 'Aisseford' Saxon English for 'Ford of the Ash',[1] is famous for its Sheepwash Bridge, a most attractive scene which appears on numerous postcards and calendars. This medieval packhorse bridge spans the River Wye and takes its name from the sheep pen by the side of it. Lambs were enclosed here while their mothers, positioned on the opposite bank, swam towards them ensuring they had a good soaking before shearing!

In the centre of the village is the *Church of the Holy Trinity* displaying reminders of earlier customs. Here, is a memorial to Henry Watson of Bakewell who, in the mid 18th century, opened the quarry of Ashford black marble at Sheldon and founded the Ashford Marble Works creating an industry of considerable local importance. Watson's father, Samuel Watson of Heanor, was 'responsible for the splendid carving at Chatsworth.'[2] Many magnificent tombs and treasures owe their grandeur to this village's industry.

Ashford has many places for refreshments. Near the bridge, and hidden behind a high stone wall, is the Riverside Country House Hotel, which provides excellent accommodation and meals in a beautiful setting. The whole village has a very rural and typically English 'olde worlde' atmosphere which attracts artists and tourists alike.

From Ashford follow the road up towards the glorious view from Monsal Head, or continue with the river downstream to Bakewell. Either destination is well worth the visit.

1. *The Derbyshire Dales.* Norman Price. F. Warne, 1953.
2. *The King's England: Derbyshire.* Arthur Mee. Hodder & Stoughton, 1974.

Ashford-in-the-Water (6 × 8) watercolour

The rough 140lb watercolour paper gave texture to this broadly painted picture. The copper beech was a strong mix of French Ultramarine with Alizarin Crimson. The basic green mix was Cadmium Yellow, Winsor Blue and Burnt Sienna-Burnt Umber. While Payne's Gray with a little Cobalt Blue, was added for the water.

- Pauline Shearstone -

MONSAL DALE
Off the B6465 near Little Longstone

From Ashford-in-the-Water, travel on to Monsal Dale where the River Wye twists and turns through the dale. The view from Monsal Head is an unforgettable sight. The railway viaduct which spans the dale may have shocked Ruskin who wrote 'now every fool in Buxton can be at Bakewell in half an hour and every fool in Bakewell at Buxton',[1] but perhaps Ruskin may have been a bit hasty in his judgement for one sees the beauty first and foremost. Closed in 1968, this old railway route is now the Monsal Trail, with numerous walks to attempt and enjoy. Monsal Head Hotel, craft centre and tea rooms offer the visitor rest and refreshment, especially welcome after ascending the steep hill from the dale below.

1. *The Derbyshire Dales*. N. Price. F. Warne, 1953.

Monsal Dale ($8 \times 5^{1}/_{2}$) watercolour

This is a favourite view of Monsal Dale with the viaduct spanning the river below. I remember seeing this view for the first time and being completely overawed by such beauty. I gave the painting a winter setting, choosing soft pink and purple colours such as Rose Madder and Cobalt Blue. The darker purples in the foreground and under the arches were a mix of Alizarin Crimson and French Ultramarine. The viaduct, the focal point of the painting, was very carefully drawn in first before an overall wash of Burnt Umber was added. The height of the background hills conveyed a feeling of depth and vastness to the painting.

-Pauline Shenstone ARA-

BAKEWELL
At the junction of the A6 and the A619

Bakewell is an attractive market town which lies on the banks of the River Wye. Monday is Market Day and as such it can be very busy. This popular place has riverside walks where ducks eagerly welcome visitors! Its ancient bridge, built with five pointed arches and widened in the 19th century, is perhaps the most painted bridge in the area! Further downstream is a little packhorse bridge, barely four feet wide.

The Saxons called the town Baeccanwyllan (the Bathing Well). The wells are of no real importance now but in the early 1700s the Duke of Rutland tried to establish a Spa here. He was unsuccessful due to the water being colder than at Buxton. The Bath House, on Bath Street, and Gardens still remain, although the bath is no longer used. Bakewell is famous for its Bakewell tart (called pudding locally). Originally made in about 1859, when a cook at the local hotel, now the *Rutland Arms*, mistakenly poured egg mixture over a strawberry tart. It was too late to correct the mistake and the sweet was served to the guests who enjoyed it so much that the Bakewell Pudding came into being.

Jane Austen stayed at the Rutland in 1811 and parts of her novel *Pride and Prejudice* can be identified with the area.

Dominating the town is *All Saints Church* mentioned in the Domesday book as having had two priests. Much of the present church is of the 14th century with the tower and spire being built in 1340. The steep walk up to the church is a form of pilgrimage by many who are attracted to the Vernon Chapel and its association with Haddon Hall, Dorothy Vernon and her husband Sir John Manners. There is so much to see in the church that you need to allow sufficient time here to fully appreciate its treasures.

In early August, a big attraction for visitors to Bakewell is the Bakewell Show, an established and renowned agricultural show. Whatever your reason for visiting this market town it does have a good variety of subjects to paint.

Bakewell (6³/₄ × 13) watercolour

-Pauline Shearstone-

Here are some useful colour mixes which you may find helpful. Paint the colours first onto 140lb NOT watercolour paper. Then cut out to form a small booklet so that you can refer to it when painting outdoors. The booklet is so much easier to use than taking A4 sheets with you.

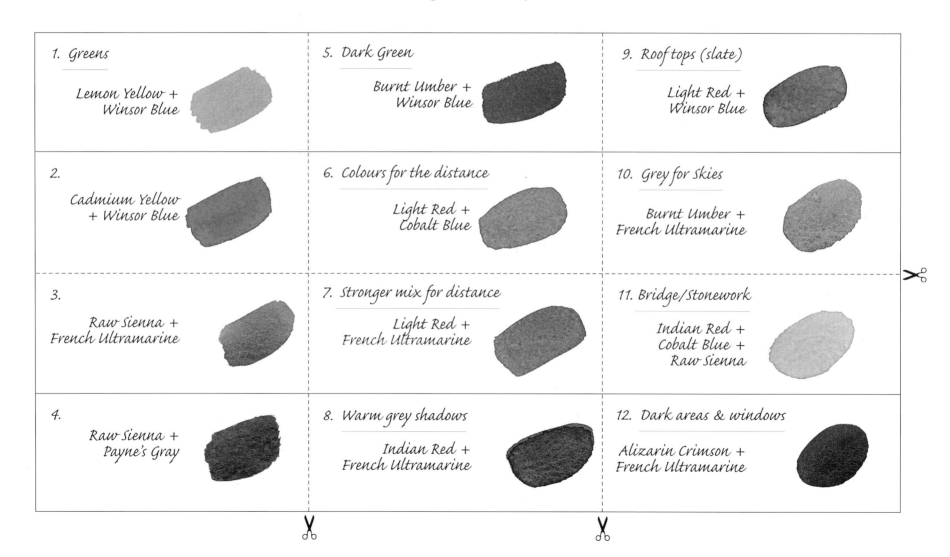

1. Greens

Lemon Yellow +
Winsor Blue

5. Dark Green

Burnt Umber +
Winsor Blue

9. Roof tops (slate)

Light Red +
Winsor Blue

2.

Cadmium Yellow
+ Winsor Blue

6. Colours for the distance

Light Red +
Cobalt Blue

10. Grey for Skies

Burnt Umber +
French Ultramarine

3.

Raw Sienna +
French Ultramarine

7. Stronger mix for distance

Light Red +
French Ultramarine

11. Bridge/Stonework

Indian Red +
Cobalt Blue +
Raw Sienna

4.

Raw Sienna +
Payne's Gray

8. Warm grey shadows

Indian Red +
French Ultramarine

12. Dark areas & windows

Alizarin Crimson +
French Ultramarine

Pauline giving an outdoor painting demonstration at Chatsworth
(Photograph A. Payne)

CONCLUSION

Having reached the end of the journey, I hope that this book has encouraged those of you who always wanted to paint in watercolours to take the first initial steps. Someone once said that 'every long journey begins with one small step'—how right they were!

For the experienced painter, I hope that you will discover new locations to paint. If you are not a painter, but have bought the book to enjoy the illustrations, then I hope that it will encourage you to visit, or revisit, the places shown and that it will enable you to see The City and The Peak District with fresh eyes.

Pauline holds various Watercolour Painting Courses throughout the year including her popular Painting in The Peak District Course.

For further details of her courses please telephone 0114 239 0197

Journey's End

Armed with a paint box, one cannot be bored, one cannot be left at a loose end, one cannot have several days on one's hands. Good gracious! What there is to admire and how little time there is to see it in! For the first time one begins to envy Methuselah.

Winston Churchill